Lightning-

German

For Kids and Families

Learn German, speak German, teach kids German – even if you don't speak a word now!

- Built around every day situations – no need to set aside special time, and you will use your new language the first day!
- Phonetic pronunciation included – no current German knowledge needed!
- Fun and easy to start!

Contents

Introduction 5

Grammar notes 7

How to use this book 9

Conversation #1: Getting dressed 13

Conversation #2: What's for breakfast? 17

Conversation #3: Ready to go? 21

Conversation #4: Where are we going? 25

Conversation #5: Comparisons / opposites 27

Conversation #6: My toys 31

Conversation #7: What's for lunch? 35

Conversation #8: A walk outside 37

Conversation #9: Want to play? 39

Conversation #10: Ouch! 41

Conversation #11: How was school today? 45

Conversation #12: Time for Dinner! 49

Conversation #13: Over, under, in, out 51

Conversation #14: Around the house 53

Conversation #15: I spy 55

Activities 57

The Map Game 59

Map Game Word List 61

Treasure Hunt 63

Scavenger Hunt #1 65

Scavenger Hunt #2 66

Scavenger Hunt #3 67

Scavenger Hunt Word Lists 68

Bingo 71

Games 73

Hokey Pokey 75

Concentration 76

Wo ist...? 76

Was ist das? 77

Twister 78

Charades 79

Recommended additional materials 81

Introduction

Like so many others, this story starts when I had children. I had been ineffectively learning Spanish for 20+ years (never got much past "mas tacos por favor"). Once the children started arriving I was focused for several years on bottles, diapers, and trying to catch up on my sleep. But once they got into school and I had a little time to read again I learned that kids who are bilingual are supposed to have an edge in life. I of course wanted the best for my crew, so I began obsessively buying language programs and trying them out on my too-young-to-complain subjects.

After a year or so of this, I was burned out with the whole concept, and my kids had pretty much achieved the ability to count to 10 in Spanish. But still I encouraged them to press on. "If we can just get to the point where we can speak to each other in Spanish, I think it will all start to come together for us! We can practice around the house, and then get comfortable enough to try it with outsiders".

And then, the light bulb finally came on. Instead of waiting for us to gain the ability to talk to each other, perhaps I could pay attention to the things we talk about, translate them into Spanish, write them down – and we could start talking to each other in Spanish right away!

Once we started using the Spanish book we got even more inspired – and I had the conversations translated into several more languages my kids wanted to learn.

And so, this book was born. We have had a lot of fun putting these together and using them, and have actually learned some foreign languages along the way.

Now it's your turn! Jump in and try them!

Grammar notes

I don't believe you need to know grammar to speak German; that will come to you as you learn and use words in context. But these are a few items that I think will help you avoid confusion as you go through the scenarios to follow...

Grammar note: gender

You probably are already aware that German nouns have "gender", and the articles (a, an, the) put before them must reflect that gender. The choice of male vs. female is not always obvious to a native English speaker, so it's important to keep the article with the word when you are memorizing it.

The masculine definite article ("the") is der, feminine is die, and neuter is das.

** This is not something to spend lots of time worrying about – once you learn enough German to converse with native speakers your pronunciation and grammar will improve rapidly. If you say a few of these things incorrectly at the beginning they will understand.

How to use this book

The fastest way to learn German is to use it! If you want your family to speak German you need to find ways to incorporate it into your everyday life.

I found the biggest obstacle to teaching my children a foreign language was time. I don't speak the language, so in order to teach I would have to first research and memorize. Somehow that just never happened.

This program is designed to eliminate that obstacle. To get started, identify a time of day or daily conversation that you think would be easiest to start with. Although the conversations are numbered one through fifteen you do not need to use them in that order. If there are particular activities or times of day that seem easier to add German to, start there. They are intended to be stand-alone, with any needed vocabulary repeated, with the exception of #15 - which is a recap of all prior lessons.

Turn to the appropriate section of the book and jump in! Any suggested preparation is noted at the beginning of the section, and there are example sentences to use right away. There are also additional vocabulary lists in each section so you can tailor the sentences to your specific situation.

Start off the conversation by reading a sentence, and acting it out as much as you can. For example, hold up a red skirt and some black pants, and ask, "Was gehört dir – der rote Rock oder die schwarze Hose?" (văs gay-hort deer – dayr rohte rŏck ŏdayr dee shvahr-tse hoh-ze)- "Which is yours – the red skirt or the black pants?" Shake or point to the skirt when you say "Rock", and to the pants when you say "Hose".

Your student will probably look at you blankly. In that case, say in English, "I'm asking you which is yours, the red skirt or the black pants". Then, repeat the question in German: "Was gehört dir – der rote Rock oder die schwarze Hose??"

They will likely now point to one or the other. This is your queue to feed them the reply you'd like – for example, say "Can you say it in German? der rote Rock?" and wait for them to repeat it. The act of speaking and the visual of you holding up the red skirt will help them remember the words.

That only took about 10 seconds! Just a few minutes each day built around visual cues and daily activities will start building your German skills.

One key to remember is that you will need to use each conversation a few times before the vocabulary becomes second nature. Rather than trying to go through the entire book at once, plan on introducing one or two conversations a week and repeat each a few times. You can start with just a few of the vocabulary words the first time through, and add a few more each time you repeat it.

You will find after a few repetitions that you won't need the notes any more, and that you and your students will be able to "ad lib" a bit.

Once you reach this point it would be good to expose your group to native speakers. Don't worry if your vocabulary is limited, most people will be happy to help you! Being around people speaking German in context will improve your skills faster than any amount of flash cards or DVDs.

It can be scary the first time you use your new German language skills in public. One way to dip your toe in the water would be to eat in a German restaurant, with a goal of communicating with your server in German. The vocabulary in the "What's for dinner" and "What's for lunch" sections will easily translate to a restaurant setting.

As a next step, so you might try going to a park or playground in an area where many native speakers live. If you have passed #9 "Want to Play" you will probably find that your children bravely walk up to other children and ask them, "Hallo, möchtest du spielen?" That's your queue to say "Hallo" to the parents as well!

The back section of the book includes fun games and activities that you can use to reinforce the German you are learning. Plug them into your study at any time you feel ready for them.

Now it's time for the most crucial step – getting started! Go ahead, pick a section, and start learning German Lightning-Fast!

Conversation #1: Getting dressed

Concepts / vocabulary introduced:

Names of clothing items
Colors
Adjectives

Preparation:

Get out a selection of clothing. Alternatively – you can start with a basket of clothes you need to sort out and get two things done at once!

The Conversation:

You will hold up two different items of clothing, and ask questions. Here are several different questions to get you started:

Welches Hemd gefällt dir besser? (vĕl-ches hĕmt gay-vĕlt deer bĕs-ser)- Which (shirt) do you like better?

Welches Hemd gehört dir? (vĕl-ches hĕmt gay-hort deer) - Which one is yours?

Magst du lieber XXX oder XXX? (măkst dōō lee-ber XXX oh-der XXX) - Do you prefer XXX or XXX?

Möchtest du lieber XXX anziehen oder XXX? (moch-tĕst dōō lee-ber XXX ăn-tsee-hen oh-der XXX) - Would you rather wear the XXX or XXX?

Ist das rot oder blau? (ĭst dăs roht oh-der blow) – Is this red or blue?

You will want to describe the objects you are holding up as part of the question. For example, I might hold up a red skirt and some black pants. I could ask my daughter, "Was gehört dir – der rote Rock oder die schwarze Hose?" (văs gay-hort deer – dayr rohte rŏck ŏdayr dee shvahr-tse hoh-ze)- "Which is yours – the red skirt or the black pants?"

When your students have memorized some of the words, you can move on to holding up a single item and ask, "Was ist das?" (văs ĭst dăs) - "What is this?" They should then answer with, "Das ist XX" (dăs ĭst) where they include some specifics about the item, for example "Das ist ein roter Rock" (dăs ĭst ein rohter rŏck)– "It's a red skirt".

Vocabulary:

Clothing:

die Bluse (dee blōō-se)- blouse
der Mantel (dayr măn-tel)- coat
das Kleid (dăs kleit)- dress
der Hut (hōōt)- hat
die Jacke (ya-cke)- jacket
die Jeans (jeans)- jeans
der Pyjama (py-yah-mah)- pajamas
die Hose (hoh-ze)- pants, trousers
die Handtasche (hănt-tăshe)- purse
das Hemd (hĕmt)- shirt
der Schuh (shōō)- shoe
die Shorts (shorts)- shorts
der Rock (rŏck)- skirt
die Socke (sŏcke)- sock
der Pullover (pullover)- sweater
das Sweatshirt (sweatshirt)- sweatshirt
der Badeanzug (bahde-ặn-tsuk)- swimsuit
die Unterwäsche (ōōn-ter-vayshe)- underwear

Colors:

gelb (gĕlb)- yellow
blau (blow)- blue
beige (beh-sh)- beige
weiß (veiss)– white

burgunder (bōōr-gōōn-der)- burgundy
grau (grow)– grey
braun (brown)– brown
violett (fī-ohlĕt)– purple
orange (oh-rănge)– orange
schwarz (shvahr-ts)– black
rot (roht)– red
rosa (roh-sah)– pink
grün (grūn)- green
aquamarin (ahkvah-mărĭn)- aqua

Adjectives:

lang (lahng) – long
kurz (kōōrts)- short
gestreift (ge-shtreift)– striped
kariert (kăreert)– plaid
gemustert (ge-mōōstert)- patterned

Conversation #2: What's for breakfast?

Concepts / vocabulary introduced:

Foods and descriptors
Numbers one to five

Preparation:

Get out some breakfast food items. The vocabulary list includes eggs, bread, toast, bacon, butter, jelly, rolls, muffins, bananas, yogurt and orange juice.

The Conversation:

First, let everyone know that:

Ich möchte gerne (ĭch moch-te gĕrne) = I would like, a polite way of asking for something

Möchtest du (moch-tĕst dōō) = Would you like?

Ja (yah) = Yes

Nein, Danke (nein, dănke) = No thank you

Mehr (mer) = More

Then for each person, stand by the choices holding their plate. You will ask them if they want something, and they will say yes or no.

For example, if you have waffles, ask "Möchtest du eine Semmel?" (moch-tĕst dōō ei-ne zĕm-mel)

They answer either "Ja, ich möchte gerne eine Semmel.", or "Nein Danke, keine Semmel.". Once you put it on their plate, ask if they would like more: "Möchtest du gerne noch eine Semmel?" And they can again answer, "Ja, ich möchte gerne eine Semmel.", or "Nein Danke, keine Semmel mehr.".

Some other sentences that may be useful:

Was gibt es zum Frühstück? (văs gĭbt ĕs tsōōm frū̆h-shtū̆ck)- What are we having for breakfast?
Ich möchte gerne XXX zum Frühstück (ĭch moch-te gĕrne XXX tsōōm frū̆h-shtū̆ck)- I would like XXX for breakfast.

Ich möchte gerne mehr XXX , bitte. (ĭch moch-te gĕrne mer XXX bĭt-te)- I would like more XXX please

Wieviele möchtest du? (vee-fee-le moch-tĕst dōō)- How many would you like?

Ich möchte gerne drei mehr XXX, bitte (ĭch moch-te gĕrne drei mer XXX bĭt-te)– I would like three more XXX please

Vocabulary:

Polite requests:

Ich möchte gerne (ĭch moch-te gĕrne) = I would like, a polite way of asking for something
Möchtest du (moch-tĕst dōō) = Would you like?
Ja (yah) = Yes
Nein, Danke (nein dănke) = No thank you

Numbers:

Eins (eins) - one
Zwei (tsvei)- two
Drei (drei)- three
Vier (feer)- four
Fünf (fū̆nf)– five

Food list:

Eier (ei-er)- Eggs
Rühreier (rṻr-ei-er)- Scrambled eggs
Speck (shpĕck)- Bacon
Toast (toast)- Toast
Scheiben Toast (shei-bĕn toast)- Pieces of toast
Brot (broht)- Bread
Scheiben Brot (shei-bĕn broht)- Pieces of bread
Butter (boo-ter)- Butter
Marmelade (mahr-mĕ-lah-de)- Jelly
Erdbeer-Marmelade (ĕrt-bĕr mahr-mĕ-lah-de)- Strawberry jelly
Eine Semmel (ei-ne zĕm-mel)- Roll
Semmeln (zĕm-meln)- Rolls
Muffin (muffin)- Muffin
Banane (bah-nă-nĕ)- Banana
Joghurt (yoh-goort)– Yogurt
Orangensaft (ohrăn-gen-zăft)– orange juice

Conversation #3: Ready to go?

Concepts / vocabulary introduced:

Getting dressed
Brushing hair
Packing lunch

Preparation:

This role play takes place just before you leave the house, so leave some extra time!

The Conversation:

You will ask if each task is completed while imitating it. By this time they should respond either "Ja" or "Nein". You will then need to feed them the appropriate full sentence answer. For example, you might say Hast du deine Zähne geputzt? Have you brushed your teeth? while making a teeth-brushing motion with your hand. The child might answer "Ja" or "Nein", or might answer "yes" or "no" in English. If they look confused, say "I am asking if you have brushed your teeth yet", and then repeat the question in German again. Once they have answered, feed them the entire answer sentence in German– either "Ja, ich habe meine Zähne geputzt" or "Nein, ich habe meine Zähne nicht geputzt", and have them repeat it.

It may feel a bit slow and cumbersome the first time through, but if you repeat a few mornings in a row it will quickly become easy.

Here are question and possible answer combinations:

¡Guten Morgen! Bist du fertig, können wir gehen? (gōō-ten mŏr-gen! bĭst dōō fĕr-tik, kon-nen veer gĕ-hen?) Good morning! Are you ready to go?
Ja, wir können gehen. (yah, veer kon-nen gĕ-hen)– Yes, I am ready to go
Nein, ich bin nicht fertig. (nein, ĭch bĭn nĭcht fĕr-tĭk)– No, I am not ready to go

Hast du deine Zähne geputzt? (hăst dōō dei-ne tsay-ne ge-pōōtzt) - Have you brushed your teeth?
Ja, ich habe meine Zähne geputzt." (yah, ĭch hă-be mei-ne tsay-ne ge-pōōtzt) - Yes, I have brushed my teeth
Nein, ich habe meine Zähne nicht geputzt. (nein, ĭch hă-be mei-ne tsay-ne nĭcht ge-pōōtzt) - No, I have not brushed my teeth

Hast du dein Haar gebürstet? (hăst dōō dein hahr ge-būrstet) - Have you brushed your hair?
Ja, ich habe mein Haar gebürstet." (yah, ĭch hă-be mein hahr ge-būrstet) – Yes, I have brushed my hair
Nein, ich habe mein Haar nicht gebürstet. (nein, ĭch hă-be mein hahr nĭcht ge-būrstet) – No, I have not brushed my hair

Hast du dein Mittagessen gemacht? (hăst dōō dein mĭt-tăk-ĕssen ge-măcht) - Have you prepared your lunch?
Ja, ich habe mein Mittagessen gemacht. (yah, ĭch hă-be mein mĭt-tăk-ĕssen ge-măcht)– Yes, I have prepared my lunch
Nein, ich habe mein Mittagessen nicht gemacht. (nein, ĭch hă-be mein mĭt-tăk-ĕssen nĭcht ge-măcht) – No, I have not prepared my lunch

Bist du angezogen? (bĭst dōō ănge-tsoh-gen) - Are you dressed?
Ja, ich bin angezogen (yah, ĭch bĭn ănge-tsoh-gen)– Yes, I am dressed
Nein, ich bin nicht angezogen (nein, ĭch bĭn nĭcht ănge-tsoh-gen) – No, I am not dressed

Hast du XXX an? (hah-st dōō XXX ăn) – Are you wearing XXX?
Ja, ich habe XXX an. (yah, ĭch hă-be XXX ăn) – Yes, I am wearing XXX
Nein, ich habe XXX nicht an. (nein, ĭch hă-be XXX nĭcht ăn)– No, I am not wearing XXX

Here are examples with some specific clothing items filled in:
Hast du ein Hemd an? (hah-st dōō ein hĕmt ăn) - Are you wearing a shirt?
Hast du eine Hose an? (hah-st dōō ei-ne hoh-ze ăn) - Are you wearing pants?
Hast du Schuhe an? (hah-st dōō shōō-he ăn) - Are you wearing shoes?
Hast du Socken an? (hah-st dōō sŏcken ăn) - Are you wearing socks?
Hast du ein Kleid an? (hah-st dōō ein kleit ăn) - Are you wearing a dress?

Conversation #4: Where are we going?

Concepts / vocabulary introduced:

Names of places
Wir müssen, or "we need"
gehen, or "to go"
Words relating to timing of events

Preparation:

Think about the errands or stops you need to make.

The Conversation:

First, discuss your errands. Start with, "Gehen wir zum" (gĕ-hen veer tsōōm)- We need to go to – and name places to go.

Examples:
Zuerst müssen wir zum Lebensmittelgeschäft gehen. – First, we need to go to the grocery store.
Später müssen wir zur Bücherei gehen. – Later, we need to go to the library.
Wir müssen bald zur Schule gehen. – We need to go to the school soon.

Have your students repeat back the planned errands, and make sure they understand what they are saying.

You can then move into some proposed other stops:

Möchtest du auch auf den Spielplatz gehen? – Would you like to go to the playground too?

Once the plan is complete – say "Gehen wir zum Auto!"(gĕ-hen veer tsōōm ow-toh)– Let's go to the car!

Vocabulary:

Timing of events:

Heute (hoi-te)- Today
Morgen (mŏr-gen)- Tomorrow
Später (shpayter)- Later
Jetzt (yĕtst)- Now
Bald (băld)- Soon
Nächste Woche (naychste vŏ-che)- Next week
In einer Woche (ĭn ei-ner vŏ-che)– In a week
Zuerst (tsōō-ĕrst)- First
Zweitens (tsvei-tens) - Second
Drittens (drĭt-tens) - Third
Viertens (feer-tens) - Fourth
Auch (owch)- Also

Places to go:

die Schule (dee shōō-le) - School
die Kirche (kĭrche)– Church
das Haus von XXX (dăs hows) – XXX's house
das Geschäft (ge-shayft)- Store
das Lebensmittelgeschäft (lĕbens-mĭt-tel-ge-shayft)– Grocery store
der Baumarkt (dayr bow-mărkt)- Hardware store
das Kaufhaus (kowf-hows)- Department store
der Park (pahrk)- Park
der Spielplatz (shpeel-plăts)- Playground
das Schwimmbad (shvĭm-băt)- Swimming pool
das Gym (gym)- Gym
die Bücherei (bŭch-erei)– Library
der Buchladen (bōōch-lăden)- Bookstore
die Tankstelle (tănk-shtĕl-le) - Gas station

Conversation #5: Comparisons / opposites

Concepts / vocabulary introduced:

Comparison words

Preparation:

Not many object names have been covered yet, so this role play works best if you walk around the house and find appropriate comparisons. You will provide the comparisons, but not try to name the objects.

The Conversation:

Walk around the house, and look for objects to compare. First you will show the comparison, and then ask the child(ren) to imitate it, as they will learn much faster if they say it themselves.

Here are suggestions:

- Go into the bathroom. Point to a wet towel (or get out a washcloth and wet it), and say "nass". Point to a dry towel and say "trocken".
- Go into a child's bedroom. Point to a stuffed toy and say "weich". Rap your knuckle on the bed frame and say "hart".
- Go into the kitchen, and fill a glass with water. Say "voll", then empty the water into the sink, hold the glass up again and say "leer".
- Point to yourself, and then hold your hand horizontally at the top of your head. Say "großer Mann" if you are a man, "große Frau" if you are a woman. Hold your hand horizontally at the height of your child's head, and say "kleiner Junge" (for a boy) or "kleines Mädchen" (for a girl). (This only works if they are shorter than

you! If not you can compare yourself to a pet or to some other shorter item)

- Point to your face, and make a big smile Say "fröhlich". Then, make a very sad face and say "traurig".
- Pull a large cooking spoon out, and say "lang". Then pull out a teaspoon and say "kurz".
- Go into the living room. Point to the sofa and say "groß". Then, point to a small object like a block, and say "klein".
- Locate 2 toy vehicles. Drive one quickly along the floor and say "schnell". Drive the second slowly, and say "langsam".
- Open a chest or box, or a door, and say "offen". Close it, and say "geschlossen".

Vocabulary:

lang (lăng) – long
kurz (kōōrts)- short
hell (hĕll)- light
dunkel (dōōn-kel)- dark
groß (grŏss)– big
klein (klein)– small
groß (grŏss)- tall
klein (klein)- short
hübsch, nett (hūbsh, nĕtt)- pretty
hässlich (hĕss-lĭch)– ugly
fröhlich (froh-lĭch)– happy
traurig (trow-rĭg)- sad
voll (fŏll)- full
leer (layr)– empty
nass (năss)– wet
trocken (trŏcken)– dry
schnell (shnĕll)– fast
langsam (lăng-săm)– slow
oben (ŏben)– up
unten (ōōn-ten)– down
dick (dĭck)– thick
dünn (dūnn)– thin
weich (veich)– soft
hart (hărt)– hard
offen (ŏf-fen)– open
geschlossen (ge-shlŏs-sen)– closed

Conversation #6: My toys

Concepts / vocabulary introduced:

Names of different objects
Continued practice on colors and comparison words

Preparation:

Select several toys to use for the role play, and make sure you know the German name for each of them.

The Conversation:

First, introduce the objects you will be using. For example, hold up a toy train and say,
Das ist ein Zug. - This is a train.

Once you've introduced several objects, ask questions and have the student point to or pick up the item you are asking about:
Suche den Zug – Look for the train
Siehst du den Zug? – Do you see the train?
Ich sehe einen Zug. – I see a train
Ich sehe einen roten Zug. – I see a red train
Welches ist der Zug? – Which is the train?

Vocabulary:

Suche (zōō-che) – Look for
Siehst du (zeest dōō) – Do you see
Ich sehe (ĭch zay-he) – I see
Welches ist (vĕl-ches ĭst) – Which is
der Zug – (dayr tsōōg) the train
das Auto – (dăs owtoh) the car
der Hubschrauber (hōōb-shrow-ber)– the helicopter
das Flugzeug (flōōg-tsoig)– the airplane

die Puppe (dee pōōp-pe)– the doll
der Ball (băll)– the ball
das Buch (bōōch)– the book
der Lastwagen (lăst-vah-gen)– the truck
das Feuerwehrauto (foier-vayr-owtoh)– the firetruck
der Bär (bayr)– the bear
die Trommel (trŏm-mel)– the drum
der Block (blŏck)– the block

More colors:

gelb (gĕlb)- yellow
blau (blow)- blue
beige (beh-sh)- beige
weiss (veiss)– white
burgundrot (bōōr-gōōnt-roht)- burgundy
braun (brown)- brown
hellbraun (hĕll-brown)- tan
gold (gŏlt)– gold
smaragdgrün (zmărăgt-grūn)– emerald
grau (grow)– grey
lila (lĭlah)– lavender
magenta (mah-gĕn-tah)– magenta
purpur (pōōr-pōōr)– purple
orange (oh-rănge)– orange
schwarz (shvahr-ts)– black
silber (zĭl-ber)– silver
rot (roht)– red
rosa (roh-sah)– pink
türkis (tūr-kĭs)- turquoise
grün (grūn)- green
aquamarin (ahkvah-mărĭn)- aqua

Refresher – comparisons:

lang (lăng) – long
kurz (kōōrts)- short
groß (grŏss)– big
klein (klein)– small

hübsch, nett (hűbsh, nĕtt)- pretty
hässlich (hĕss-lĭch)– ugly
voll (fŏll)- full
leer (layr)– empty
schnell (shnĕll)– fast
langsam (lăng-săm)– slow
oben (ŏben)– up
unten (ōōnten)– down
weich (veich)– soft
hart (hărt)– hard

Conversation #7: What's for lunch?

Concepts / vocabulary introduced:

Foods and descriptors

Preparation:

Set out ingredients to make sandwiches, and also some fruit or carrots if you have them available. Also set out some plates and silverware.

The Conversation:

First, teach a few statements that will be used regularly going forward:
Was gibt es zu Mittag? (văs gĭbt ĕs tsōō mĭt-tăk)- What are we having for lunch?
Ich möchte gerne XXX zum Mittagessen. (ĭch moch-te gĕrne XXX tsōōm mĭt-tăk-ĕs-sen)– I would like XXX for lunch.

Then for the role play, explain that they will each be putting together their own sandwich. They will need to ask for each ingredient they need.

"Bitte, gib mir XXX" (bĭt-te, gĭb mĭr XXX)– Please pass the XXX
"Hier ist XXX" (heer ĭst XXX)– Here is the XXX

Vocabulary:

<u>Refresher:</u>

Ich möchte gerne (ĭch moch-te gĕrne) = I would like, a polite way of asking for something
Möchtest du (moch-tĕst dōō) = Would you like?
Ja (yah) = Yes
Nein, Danke. (nein, dănke) = No thank you

<u>Food list:</u>

das Brot (broht)–bread
das Vollkornbrot (fŏll-kŏrn-broht)- Whole Wheat bread
das Weißbrot (veiss-broht)- White bread
die Mayonnaise (may-oh-nay-se)- Mayonnaise
der Senf (zĕnf)- Mustard
der Truthahn (trōōt-hahn)- Turkey
der Käse (kayse)- Cheese
der Hartkäse (hărt-kayse)- Cheddar cheese
der Emmentalerkäse (ĕm-mĕn-tahler-kayse)- Swiss cheese
das belegte Brot (dăs bĕ-lĕgte broht)- Sandwich
der Apfel (ăpfel)- Apple
die Orange (oh-rănge)- Orange
die Banane (bah-nă-nĕ)– banana
die Erdbeeren (ĕrt-bĕren)- Strawberries
die Blaubeeren (blow-bĕren)- Blueberries
die Karotten (kah-rŏtten)- Carrots
das Teller (tĕl-ler) - Plate
das Messer (mĕs-ser)- Knife

Conversation #8: A walk outside

Concepts / vocabulary introduced:

Names of items you will see in a walk around the block

Preparation:

None! Just your vocabulary lists if you need them at hand.

The Conversation:

For this role play you will just take a walk and point out things you see. You and the students can incorporate comparison words and colors into your discussion.

Here are some examples:

Das ist ein Zaun. (dăs ĭst ein tsown)- This is a fence
Welche Farbe hat der Zaun? (vĕl-che fărbe hăt dayr tsown) - What color is the fence?
Der Zaun ist rot. (dayr tsown ĭst roht)- The fence is red.
Siehst du einen Stein? (zĭst dōō ei-nen shtein) - Do you see a rock?
Ist der Stein groß oder klein? (ĭst dayr shtein grŏss ŏder klein) - Is the rock big or small?
Der Stein ist klein. (dayr shtein ĭst klein) - The rock is small.
Ist das Gras lang oder kurz? (ĭst dăs grăs lăng ŏder kōōrts) - Is the grass long or short?
Das Gras ist lang. (dăs grăs ĭst lăng) - The grass is tall.

Vocabulary:

der Baum (bowm)- Tree
die Blume (blōō-me) - Flower

die Blumen (blōō-men) - Flowers
der Busch (bōōsh)- Bush
das Gras (grăs)- Grass
der Stein (shtein)- Rock
die Erde (ĕrde)- Dirt
der Schmetterling (shmĕt-ter-lĭng)- Butterfly
der Käfer (kay-fer)- Beetle
die Ameise (ămeise)- Ant
der Vogel (fŏgel) - Bird
das Eichhörnchen (eich-horn-chen)- Squirrel
der Hund (hōōnt)- Dog
die Katze (kătse)- Cat
der Zaun (tsown)- Fence
das Auto (ow-toh) - Car
der Lastwagen (lăst-vah-gen)- Truck
das Motorrad (mŏtŏr-răt) - Motorcycle
das Fahrrad (fahr-răt)– Bicycle
der Telefonmast (tĕlĕ-fŏn-măst)- Telephone pole
die Zufahrt (tsu-fahrt)– Driveway
die Straße (shtrăsse)- Street
der Gehsteig (gĕh-shteig)- Sidewalk
der Postkasten (pŏst-kăsten)- Mailbox

Conversation #9: Want to play?

Concepts / vocabulary introduced:

Would you like to play?
Names of games and sports
Playground equipment

Preparation:

This one works best if you go to a playground and bring along some sports equipment.

The Conversation:

Explain to the student that they are going to pretend they have just met a new friend at the park and want to play with them. Have them practice the sentences a few times, then they should pretend you are their new friend and say “Hallo, möchtest du spielen?” They can then try asking what their new friend likes to do, and finally suggest an activity.

Hallo (hăllŏ)– Hi
Möchtest du spielen? (moch-tĕst dōō shpee-len)- Would you like to play?
Magst du XXX? (măgst dōō XXX)- Do you like XXX?
Kann ich auch spielen? (kănn ĭch owch shpee-len)- Can I play too?
Spielen wir XXX (Shpee-len veer XXX)- Let’s play XXX
Gehen wir zu XXX (gay-hen veer tsōō XXX)- Let’s go to XXX
Laß uns XXX (lăss ōōns XXX)– Let’s XXX (a verb, like “let’s jump”)

Vocabulary:

<u>Games:</u>
Tennis (tĕn-nĭs)- Tennis

Fußball (fōōss-băll)- Soccer
Basketball (băsket-băll)- Basketball
Baseball (base-băll)– Baseball

<u>Equipment:</u>
die Schaukel (show-kel)- Swing
die Rutsche (rōōtshe)- Slide
der Sandkasten (zănt-kăsten)- Sandbox
der Ball (băll)– Ball
der Drachen (drăchen)– Kite

<u>Activities:</u>
gehen (gay-hen)– to walk
laufen (lowfen)– to run
springen (shprĭngen)– to jump
klettern (klĕttern)– to climb
einen Ball schießen (ei-nen băll sheessen)– to kick
werfen (vĕrfen)– to throw
Laß uns laufen (lăss ōōns lowfen) - Let's run
Laß uns springen (lăss ōōns shprĭngen) - Let's jump
Laß uns klettern (lăss ōōns klĕttern) - Let's climb
Laß uns mit XXX spielen (lăss ōōns mĭt XXX shpee-len) - Let's play with XX
Laß uns auf XXX spielen (lăss ōōns owf XXX shpee-len) - Let's play on XXX

Conversation #10: Ouch!

Concepts / vocabulary introduced:

Parts of the body

Preparation:

None needed

The Conversation:

Children usually have more fun with learning body parts if you can make it silly. For example, pretend to trip, and stand up holding part of your body and say "¡Autsch! Mein Arm tut weh!" (owtsh! mein ărm tōōt vayh) (Ouch, I hurt my arm). Then point to the arm, and say "der Arm" and have your students repeat it while pointing to their own arm. You can also bring in an ice pack, and pretend to put it on the hurting spot, then pass it to the student.

You also can go over a few parts of the body with them, then say "Was ist das?" (văs ĭst dăs) (What is this?) while pointing to a part of the body to test their knowledge.

And, finally here is a translation of the "hokey pokey" song you can sing. Stand in a circle, and substitute a body part for the __:

Gib ____ hinein (gĭb _ hĭn-ein) (die Hand, for example) (put the part inside the circle)

Nimm ____ heraus (nĭmm _ hĕr-ows) (put the part outside the circle)

Gib ____ hinein und man schüttelt sie heraus (gĭb _ hĭn-ein ōōnt măn shṻttĕlt zee hĕr-ows) (put the part inside the circle and shake it)

Du singst den Hokey Pokey und du drehst dich um dich selbst (dōō zingst dĕn hokey pokey ōōnt dōō drayst dĭch ōōm dĭch zelbst) (turn in a circle)

Das ist's worum es geht. (dăs ĭsts vŏ-rōōm ĕs gayt) (clap your hands with this part)

Vocabulary:

der Arm (ărm)- arm
der Rücken(rṻcken)- back
die Wirbelsäule (vĭrbel-sayle)- backbone
das Gehirn (gĕ-hĭrn) - brain
die Brust (brōōst)- chest
der Hintern (hĭn-tern) - buttocks
die Wade (va-de)- calf
das Ohr (ohr)- ear
der Ellbogen (ĕll-bŏgen)- elbow
das Auge (ow-ge)- eye
der Finger (fĭn-ger)- finger
der Fuß (fōōss)- foot
das Haar (hahr)- hair
die Hand (hănt)- hand
der Kopf (kŏpf)- head
das Herz (hĕrts)- heart
die Hüfte (hṻfte)- hip
das Knie (k-nee)- knee
das Bein (bein)- leg
der Mund (mōōnt)- mouth
der Muskel (mōōskel)- muscle
der Hals (hăls)- neck
die Nase (nahse)- nose

die Schulter (shōōl-ter)- shoulder
die Haut (howt)- skin
der Bauch (bowch)- stomach (abdomen)
der Oberschenkel (obayr-shĕnkel)- thigh
die Kehle, der Rachen (kĕh-le, răchen)- throat
die Zehe (tsay-he)- toe
die Zunge (tsōōnge)- tongue
der Zahn (tsahn)- tooth

Conversation #11: How was school today?

Concepts / vocabulary introduced:

Words relating to common school activities.

Preparation:

You will want to get a few props together relating to the activities you are going to ask about. For example, have a paint brush handy if you are going to ask about painting. Have a story book at hand to ask about reading.

The Conversation:

First you will ask, "Was hast du heute in der Schule gemacht?" (văs hăst dōō hoi-te ĭn dayr shōō-le ge-mächt) - What did you do at school today?

Then, you will ask specific questions, while pretending to do the activity. There may be some cases which don't role play very well – then you can ask the question, then translate into English, then ask again.

For example, you might say Hast du draußen gespielt? (hăst dōō drowssen ge-shpeelt) Did you play outside? The child might answer "Ja" or "Nein". Once they have answered, feed them the entire answer sentence in German – either "Ja, ich habe draußen gespielt." (yah, ĭch hăbe drowssen ge-shpeelt) or "Nein, ich habe nicht draußen gespielt." (nein, ĭch hăbe nĭcht drowssen ge-shpeelt), and have them repeat it.

Vocabulary:

Here are question and possible answer combinations:

Hast du eine Geschichte gelesen? (hăst dōō ei-ne gĕshĭchte ge-lĕsen)- Did you read a story?
Ja, ich habe eine Geschichte gelesen. (yah, ĭch hăbe ei-ne gĕshĭchte ge-lĕsen)- Yes, I read a story
Nein, ich habe keine Geschichte gelesen. (nein, ĭch hăbe kei-ne gĕshĭchte ge-lĕsen)- No, I did not read a story

Hast du draußen gespielt? (hăst dōō drowssen ge-shpeelt) - Did you play outside?
Ja, ich habe draußen gespielthe jugado fuera (yah, ĭch hăbe drowssen ge-shpeelt) – Yes, I played outside
Nein, ich habe nicht draußen gespielt. (nein, ĭch hăbe nĭcht drowssen ge-shpeelt)– No, I did not play outside

Hast du mit XXX gespielt? (hăst dōō mĭt XXX ge-shpeelt) - Did you play with XXX? (person's name)
Ja, ich habe mit XXX gespielt. (yah, ĭch hăbe mĭt XXX ge-shpeelt)– Yes, I played with XXX
Nein, ich habe nicht mit XXX gespielt. (nein, ĭch hăbe nĭcht mĭt XXX ge-shpeelt) – No, I did not play with XXX

Hast du gemalt? (hăst dōō ge-mălt)- Did you paint?
Ja, ich habe gemalt. (yah, ĭch hăbe ge-mălt)– Yes, I painted
Nein, ich habe nicht gemalt. (nein, ĭch hăbe nĭcht ge-mălt)– No, I did not paint

Hast du geschrieben? (hăst dōō ge-shree-ben)- Did you write?
Ja, ich habe geschrieben. (yah, ĭch hăbe ge-shree-ben)– Yes, I wrote
Nein, ich habe nicht geschrieben. (nein, ĭch hăbe nĭcht ge-shree-ben) – No, I did not write

Hast du ein Bild gezeichnet? (hăst dōō ein bĭlt ge-tseich-nĕt)- Did you draw a picture?
Ja, ich habe ein Bild gezeichnet. (yah, ĭch hăbe ein bĭlt ge-tseich-nĕt)– Yes, I drew a picture
Nein, ich habe kein Bild gezeichnet. (nein, ĭch hăbe kein bĭlt ge-tseich-nĕt)– No, I did not draw a picture

Hast du einen Test gehabt? (hăst dōō ei-nen tĕst ge-hăbt) - Did you take a test?

Ja, ich habe einen Test gehabt. (yah, ĭch hăbe ei-nen tĕst ge-hăbt)– Yes, I took a test
Nein, ich habe keinen Test gehabt. (nein, ĭch hăbe kei-nen tĕst ge-hăbt)– No, I did not take a test

Hast du zu Mittag gegessen? (hăst dōō tsōō mĭt-tăk ge-gĕssen)- Did you eat lunch?
Ja, ich habe zu Mittag gegessen. (yah, ĭch hăbe tsōō mĭt-tăk ge-gĕssen) – Yes, I ate lunch
Nein, ich habe nicht zu Mittag gegessen. (nein, ĭch hăbe nĭcht tsōō mĭt-tăk ge-gĕssen) – No, I did not eat lunch

Timing of events:

You can also add some timing words to the end of your questions:

Heute (hoi-te)– today
diesen Morgen (dee-zen mŏr-gen) - this morning
diesen Nachmittag (dee-zen năch-mĭt-tăk) - this afternoon
vor der Schule (fohr dayr shōō-le)– before school
während der Pause (vayrend dayr powse) - during recess
nach der Schule (năch dayr shōō-le) - after school

Conversation #12: Time for Dinner!

Concepts / vocabulary introduced:

Polite requests
Some food names
Plate, silverware, glass

Preparation:

Select and prepare a dinner with several choices in it. The vocabulary list in this role play is designed around a chicken dinner. You may also need to look up a few ingredients, if you have different options than we use. Write down any items you offer that we don't include, and then go to Translate.Google.com, type in the word, and have it give you the German equivalent. Make a small cheat sheet for yourself if you need it.

You will need to have the food items arranged on the counter ready to serve. Each person will need to select what they want and answer questions about each of the possible choices.

The Conversation:

First, when the family comes to dinner, say "Willkommen in der deutschen Küche!" (vĭll-kŏmmen ĭn dayr doitshen kŭche)

Let them know that:

> Ich möchte gerne (ĭch moch-te gĕrne) = I would like, a polite way of asking for something
>
> Möchtest du (moch-tĕst dōō) = Would you like?
>
> Ja (yah) = Yes
>
> Nein, Danke. (nein, dănke) = No thank you

mehr (mĕr) = More

Then for each person, stand by the ingredients holding their plate.

First, point to the roast chicken and steak. Ask them, "Möchtest du Brathuhn oder Steak?"(moch-tĕst dōō braht-hōōhn ŏdayr steak)

Once they have selected, put it on the plate.

Then go through the choices, and they answer yes or no to each.

For example, if you have green beans, ask "Möchtest du Fisolen?" (moch-tĕst dōō fĭ-zohlen)

They answer either "Ja, ich möchte gerne Fisolen", or "Nein Danke, keine Fisolen". Once you put a spoonful on their plate, ask if they would like more: "Möchtest du mehr Fisolen?" And they can again answer, "Ja, ich möchte mehr Fisolen", or "Nein, Danke".

You may also ask if they would like a drink, "Möchtest du ein Glas XX?"

They answer either "Ja, ich möchte gerne ein Glas XXX", or "Nein, Danke".

<u>Vocabulary:</u>

Brathuhn (braht-hōōhn) = roast chicken
Steak (steak) = steak
Wurst (vōōrst) = sausage
Fisolen (fĭ-zohlen) = green beans
Karotten (kă-rŏt-ten) = carrots
Salat (zălăt)= salad
Soße (zohsse) = gravy
Röstkartoffeln (rost-kărtŏffeln) = roast potatoes
Kartoffelpüree (kărtŏffel-pūray) = mashed potatoes
Brot (broth) = bread
Milch (mĭlch)= milk
Wasser (văs-ser)= water
Apfelsaft (apfel-zăft) = apple juice
Glas (glahs) = glass
Kuchen (kōō-chen) = pie
Suppe (zōōppe) = soup

Conversation #13: Over, under, in, out

Concepts / vocabulary introduced:

Words describing location

Preparation:

You will need a toy (I use a bear in my examples), and a large box (big enough for you to step into).

The Conversation:

You will show the comparison using the bear or box, and then ask the child(ren) to imitate it, as they will learn much faster if they say it themselves.

Here are suggestions:

- Lift up the bear, and say "Der Bär ist oben." (the bear is up). Put it down, and say "Der Bär ist unten." (the bear is down).
- Hold the bear over the box, and say "Der Bär ist über der Schachtel." (the bear is over the box). Then, lift up the box and hold the bear under it, and say "Der Bär ist unter der Schachtel." (the bear is under the box).
- Climb inside the box, and say "Ich bin in der Schachtel." (I am inside the box). Then climb back out and say "Ich bin außerhalb der Schachtel." (I am outside the box).

- Stand behind the box, and say "Ich bin hinter der Schachtel." (I am behind the box). Move to the side of it, and say "Ich bin neben der Schachtel." (I am next to the box). Stand in front of it, and say "Ich bin vor der Schachtel." (I am in front of the box).

Then, move on to questions: Wo ist der Bär? (Where is the bear?).

Vocabulary:

oben (oh-ben)– Up
unten (ōōn-ten)– Down
über (ǖber)- Over
unter(ōōn-ter)- Under
in (ĭn)- Inside
außerhalb (owsser-hălb)– Outside
neben(nĕ-ben)– To the side
hinter (hĭn-ter)– Behind
vor (fohr)– In front of

Conversation #14: Around the house

Concepts / vocabulary introduced:

Names of common household items

Preparation:

None needed.

The Conversation:

You will walk around the house, and point to or touch items and name them. Then, the child(ren) should imitate. Once you've named the object, describe it using some of the words from prior lessons.

For example, walk up to the wall, rap on it with your knuckles, and say "Wand". Once your students imitate that, describe the wall, for example "weisse Wand" (white wall) and have them repeat.

Once you've covered the vocabulary, go around again, point to objects and say Was ist das? (văs ĭst dăs) – which means, "What is this?" – to check what your students remember.

Vocabulary:

der Dachboden (dăch-boh-den)- attic
der Keller (kĕl-ler) - basement
das Badezimmer (bahdĕ-tsĭm-mer)- bathroom
das Schlafzimmer (shlăf- tsĭm-mer) - bedroom
der Kasten (kăsten) - closet
der Hof (hohf) - courtyard

das Studierzimmer (shtōōdeer- tsĭm-mer)- den, study
das Esszimmer (ĕss- tsĭm-mer) - dining room
der Korridor (kŏrrĭ-dŏr)- entryway
das Kinderzimmer (kĭnter- tsĭm-mer)- nursery room
die Garage (gah-rahsh) - garage
die Küche (kǖche)- kitchen
das Wohnzimmer (vohn- tsĭm-mer) - living room
das Zimmer (tsĭm-mer) - room
die Decke (dĕcke)- ceiling
der Schrank (shrănk)- cabinet
die Tür (tǖr) - door
die Steckdose (shtĕck-dŏse)- electrical socket
der Wasserhahn (văs-ser-hahn) - faucet
der Boden (boh-den)(floor that is walked on), der Stock (shtŏck) (level of a building) - floor
die Küchenanrichte (kǖchen-ănrĭchte)- (kitchen) counter
die Lampe (lămpe) - lamp
das Licht (lĭcht)- light
der Spiegel (shpee-gel) - mirror
das Dach (dăch) - roof
die Spüle (shpǖ-le)- sink
die Treppe, Stiege (trĕp-pe, shtee-ge) - stairs
die Wand (vănt) - wall
das Fenster (fĕnster)- window
das Bett (bĕtt) - bed
der Stuhl, Sessel (shtōōl, zĕssel) - chair
die Kommode (kŏm-mŏde) - chest of drawers
das Sofa (zo-fah) - sofa
der Tisch (tĭsh) - table

Conversation #15: I spy

Concepts / vocabulary introduced:

This is a review of things you have worked on in prior lessons.

Preparation:

None needed.

The Conversation:

Ich sehe etwas (ĭch zĕ-he ĕtvăs) – I see something

Walk around the house, looking for items you've previously used in your role plays. Once you spot something, say " Ich sehe etwas" (ĭch zĕ-he ĕtvăs)– I see something – and then something about the item you are looking at. For example, if you see a train which is green, you would say "Ich sehe etwas grünes " (ĭch zĕ-he ĕtvăs grūnĕs), and then the correct answer would be "ein Zug" – a train.

....

Some of the things you can look for are:

- Foods or dishes in the kitchen
- Clothing in the bedrooms
- Furniture items
- Toys

Activities

The Map Game

To play, look at the map and follow the directions. Once you solve these, make up your own to share! As a next step, get out a map of your city or country and write down directions for another person to solve.

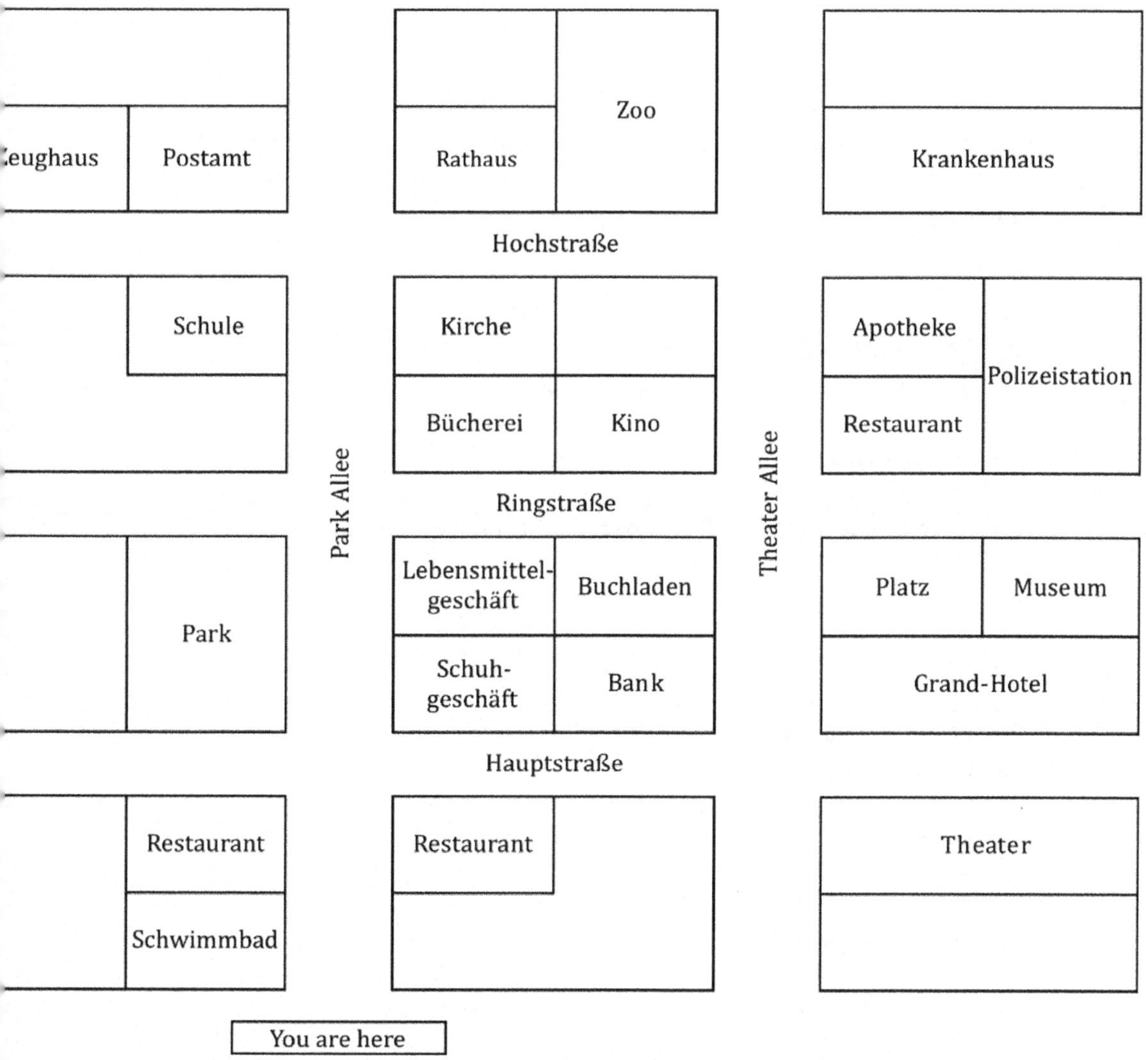

Route #1:

Directions:

Zwei Häuserblöcke geradeaus gehen.
Rechts abbiegen.
Zwei Häuserblöcke geradeaus gehen.
Dein Ziel ist rechts.

Wo bist du angekommen?

Now, give directions to go from that location to the zoo.

Route #2:

Directions:

Drei Häuserblöcke geradeaus gehen.
Dein Ziel ist links an der Straßenkreuzung.

Wo bist du angekommen?

Now, give directions to go from that location to the pharmacy.

Route #3:

Directions:

Einen Häuserblock geradeaus gehen.
Rechts abbiegen.
Einen Häuserblock geradeaus gehen.
Links abbiegen.
Dein Ziel ist links.

Wo bist du angekommen?

Now, give directions to go from that location to the police station.

Map Game Word List

Where is (the)...? Wo ist...?
It's... Es ist...

<u>Locations:</u>
bank – die Bank
bookstore – der Buchladen
church – die Kirche
city hall – das Rathaus
fire station – das Zeughaus, Feuerwehrhaus
grocery store – das Lebensmittelgeschäft
hospital – das Krankenhaus
hotel – das Hotel
library – die Bücherei
movie theater – das Kino
museum – das Museum
park – der Park
pharmacy – die Apotheke
police station – die Polizeistation
post office – das Postamt
restaurant – das Restaurant
school – die Schule
shoe store – das Schuhgeschäft
swimming pool – das Schwimmbad
theater – das Theater
zoo – der Zoo

<u>Distances, directions:</u>
der Kilometer, die Meile, der Meter — kilometer, mile, meter
die Straße, Allee, Autobahn — street, avenue, highway
der Häuserblock — city block
die Straßenecke — street corner
die Adresse — address
abbiegen - turn
umkehren - turn around
die Ampel - the traffic lights
die Kreuzung - the intersection
der Platz - the square
entgegengesetzt - opposite

hinter - behind
vor - in front of
an dieser Straße - along this street
rechts/nach rechts - on/to the right
links/nach links - on/to the left
geradeaus - go straight ahead
am/zum Ende - at/to the end
bis - up to/as far as
an der Ecke - at the corner
Es ist auf/in - it is on/in
Nord - North
Süd - South
Ost - East
West - West

Treasure Hunt

1. Get several pieces of paper or index cards, and put together clues that lead from place to place.

2. Decide what the prize will be at the end of the hunt. It does not have to be anything fancy – the chance to go on the treasure hunt will be fun in itself – but a prize is fun, perhaps some stickers, or have it end at your car and take everyone to the park.

3. Hand your students the first clue, and see how they do! If your students do not read yet – walk with them and read each clue for them as they find it.

Here are some sample clues with translations.

Look under __'s bed	Schau unter __s Bett
Look under __'s pillow	Schau unter __s Kissen
Look inside the refrigerator	Schau in den Kühlschrank
Look where we keep the milk	Schau wo wir die Milch haben
Look in the bathroom	Schau im Badezimmer
Look in the bathtub	Schau in der Badewanne
Look under the bathroom rug	Schau unter dem Badvorleger
Look under the sofa	Schau unter dem Sofa
Look next to the red chair	Schau neben dem roten Sessel

Look at the kitchen table	Schau zum Küchentisch
Look in your top dresser drawer	Schau in der obersten Kommodenlade
Look inside __'s closet	Schau in __s Schrank
Look under the kitchen sink	Schau unter der Küchenspüle
Look under the bathroom sink	Schau unter dem Waschbecken im Bad
Look on __'s desk	Schau auf __s Schreibtisch
Look above the fireplace	Schau über dem Kamin
Look inside the dishwasher	Schau im Geschirrspüler
Look near the front door	Schau bei der Eingangstür
Look near the garage door	Schau beim Garagentor
Look in the laundry room	Schau im Wäscheraum
Look near the car	Schau beim Auto
Look at the top of the stairs	Schau oberhalb der Stiege
Look at the bottom of the stairs	Schau unterhalb der Stiege
Look in the hall closet	Schau im Kasten im Vorraum
Look on top of the refrigerator	Schau auf dem Kühlschrank
Look near your shoes	Schau bei deinen Schuhen

Scavenger Hunt #1

Try to find each of the following items:

eine Sicherheitsnadel

eine Papierklammer

einen Schlüssel

ein Buch

eine CD

ein Papiertaschentuch

ein Telefon

einen Umschlag

eine Briefmarke

ein Gummiband

eine Zeitung

ein Magazin

ein Photo

eine Schachtel

einen Kugelschreiber

Scavenger Hunt #2

Try to find each of the following items:

eine Zahnbürste

eine Haarbürste

einen Bleistift

eine Haarklammer

eine Tube Klebstoff

einen Pinsel

eine Socke

einen Schuh

eine Puppe

ein Spielzeugauto

ein Plüschtier

einen Buntstift

eine Schere

ein Klebeband

einen Ball

Scavenger Hunt #3

Try to find each of the following items:

ein Hemd

einen Hut, eine Kappe

einen Löffel

eine Gabel

eine Tasse

einen Messbecher

eine kleine Schüssel

einen Kräcker

eine Frucht

ein Blatt

eine Blume

einen Grashalm

einen kleinen Stein

eine kleine Schaufel

einen Eimer

Scavenger Hunt Word Lists

#1:

die Sicherheitsnadel	safety pin
die Papierklammer	paper clip
der Schlüssel	key
das Buch	book
die CD	CD
das Papiertaschentuch	tissue
das Telefon	telephone
der Umschlag	envelope
die Briefmarke	stamp
das Gummiband	rubber band
die Zeitung	newspaper
das Magazin	magazine
das Photo	photograph
die Schachtel	box
der Kugelschreiber	pen

#2:

die Zahnbürste	toothbrush
die Haarbürste	hairbrush
der Bleistift	pencil
die Haarklammer	hair clip
der Klebstoff	glue
der Pinsel	paintbrush
die Socke	sock
der Schuh	shoe
die Puppe	doll
das Spielzeugauto	toy car
das Plüschtier	stuffed animal
der Buntstift	crayon
die Schere	scissors
das Klebeband	tape
der Ball	ball

#3:

das Hemd	shirt
der Hut, die Kappe	hat
der Löffel	spoon
die Gabel	fork
die Tasse	cup
der Messbecher	measuring cup
die kleine Schüssel	small bowl
der Kräcker	cracker
die Frucht	fruit
das Blatt	leaf
die Blume	flower
der Grashalm	blade of grass
der kleine Stein	small rock
die kleine Schaufel	small shovel
der Eimer	bucket

Bingo

To play bingo you can make up cards in advance, or you can have the players make their own cards as a first step.

Create a blank card template and a list of vocabulary words – at least 8 for a 3 x 3 card, 16 for a 4 x 4 card, or 24 for a 5 x 5 card. Pass out a vocabulary list and each person can write in their choice of words in the squares on their card – no blank spaces or repeated words.

To play, call out vocabulary words and the players mark off that word on their card. In traditional bingo the first person to get a complete row, column, or corner to corner line completed wins. In blackout bingo the first person to mark off all their squares wins.

Games

Hokey Pokey

This is a great game to use to reinforce the name of different body parts.

Here is the song in German:

Gib ____ hinein (gĭb _ hĭn-ein) (die Hand, for example)
Nimm ____ heraus (nĭmm _ hĕr-ows)
Gib ____ hinein und man schüttelt sie heraus (gĭb _ hĭn-ein ōōnt măn shūttĕlt zee hĕr-ows)
Du singst den Hokey Pokey und du drehst dich um dich selbst (dōō zingst dĕn hokey pokey ōōnt dōō drayst dĭch ōōm dĭch zelbst)
Das ist's worum es geht. (dăs ĭsts vŏ-rōōm ĕs gayt)

And, some body parts you can use:

der Arm (ărm)- arm
der Rücken(rūcken)- back
die Brust (brōōst)- chest
die Wade (va-de)- calf
das Ohr (ohr)- ear
der Ellbogen (ĕll-bŏgen)- elbow
das Auge (ow-ge)- eye
der Finger (fĭn-ger)- finger
der Fuß (fōōss)- foot
das Haar (hahr)- hair
die Hand (hănt)- hand
der Kopf (kŏpf)- head
die Hüfte (hūfte)- hip
das Knie (k-nee)- knee
das Bein (bein)- leg
der Mund (mōōnt)- mouth
der Hals (hăls)- neck
die Nase (nahse)- nose
die Schulter (shōōl-ter)- shoulder
der Oberschenkel (obayr-shĕnkel)- thigh
die Kehle, der Rachen (kĕh-le, răchen)- throat
die Zehe (tsay-he)- toe
die Zunge (tsōōnge)- tongue

Concentration

To play concentration, you will need a set of cards with 2 cards for each specific picture or word. You lay the cards upside down, and turn over 2 at a time. If the 2 match – you keep them. If not, you turn them back over and the next person gets their turn. If you pay close attention you will be able to remember where some items are as you go along, increasing your matches. The quickest way to begin playing is to purchase 2 identical sets of German flash cards and shuffle them together.

To reinforce German vocabulary, instead of having 2 matching cards – have sets of a picture and the name of that item in German, or sets with the word in German on one card and in English on the other. Then, you need to remember the vocabulary to get a match. Start with a list of vocabulary words you'd like to practice, and write the German and English words on index cards.

Wo ist...?

Wo ist...? (voh ĭst) means, "Where is?". This can be used around the house by naming specific objects or rooms, or outside by naming types of buildings or other items you might see, like a tree or bench.

Was ist das?

Was ist das? (văs ĭst dăs) means, "What is this?" It's good for pointing at objects to see if others can correctly name them in German. Use it with objects around the house or body parts. I have a friend who has taped index cards to various items in her house to help her remember them – "die Tür" on the door for example – you may want to try this as well!

Twister

Twister can be played with a twister board from the game, or you can make your own playing area by placing colored pieces of paper on the ground. To play, one person calls out the instructions which the others follow. You can use a twister spinner to select them, or assign numbers on a pair of dice (one represents color, one represents body part), or just call out what you like! The last one to fall over wins!

Example calls:

Zeige mit deiner rechten Hand auf die Farbe blau. (tseige mĭt dei-ner rĕchten hănt owf dee făr-be blow)– put your right hand on the color blue

Zeige mit deinem linken Fuß auf die Farbe orange. (tseige mĭt dei-nem lĭn-ken fōōss owf dee făr-be oh-ränge)– put your left foot on the color orange

Words you may need:

links (lĭnks) - left
rechts (rĕchts) - right
Hand (hănt) - hand
Fuß (fōōss) - foot
Kopf (kŏpf) - head
rot (roht) - red
orange (oh-rănge)– orange
gelb (gĕlb) - yellow
grün (grūn) - green
blau (blow)–blue
schwarz (shvahr-ts) - black
weiss (veiss) - white

Charades

A fun game to play with children is similar to charades. Each person takes a turn pretending to be an animal. The person who correctly guesses the animal and names it in German gets to go next!

Here's a list of animal names to get you started:

der Elch (ĕlch)— elk, moose
das Pferd (pfĕrt)— horse
das Kamel (kah-mĕl)— camel
das Kängaru (kayn-gă-rōō)— kangaroo
das Zebra (tse-bră)— zebra
das Schwein (shvein)— pig
der Schimpanse (shim-păn-se)— chimpanzee
der Hirsch (hĭrsh)— deer
der Hase (hahse)- rabbit
der Elefant (ĕlĕ-fănt)— elephant
der Seehund (zay-hōōnt)— seal
die Katze (kătse)- cat
der Gorilla (gŏril-lah)— gorilla
der Gepard (gĕpărt)— cheetah
die Giraffe (gĭraffe)— giraffe
das Nilpferd (nĭl-pfĕrt)— hippopotamus
der Koala (kŏah-lă)— koala
der Löwe (lo-ve)— lion
der Seelöwe (zay-love)— sea lion
der Leopard (lĕŏ-părt)— leopard
der Affe (ăffe)— monkey
der Bär (bayr)— bear
der Hund (hōōnt)- dog
das Nashorn (nahs-hŏrn)— rhinoceros
der Tiger (tĭ-ger)— tiger
der Fuchs (fōōchs)— fox

Recommended additional materials

None of these items are necessary, however we have found them to be fun!

Songs for the car:

A great source for traditional German children's songs is ingeb.org/nurseryr.html, where you can find the lyrics and melody for Kinderlieder.

http://german.about.com/library/blmusik_kinder.htm provides lyrics and the English translation, as well as a wealth of other German material for avid students.

A CD "German Children's Songs by Ernst Wolff", as well as an MP3 Download "Die schönsten deutschen Kinderlieder" by Die Kindergarten Kids are great add-ons to play in the car as you run errands!

Children's story books in German:

Simple children's books will have commonly used words and pictures to help with understanding, and are a great complement to the role plays. Check out what's available in your local library!

A great online source for this material is http://www.german-bookworld.com/
and http://www.alphabet-garten.com/.

German Children's DVDs:

I have not found many US DVDs with a German soundtrack, so you would likely need to purchase them online from a German language store. Please keep in mind that DVDs originating from Europe will require a multi-region DVD player.

CPSIA information can be obtained at www.ICGtesting.com
Printed in the USA
LVOW03s2007160415

434885LV00012B/216/P

9 781470 132804